MILNER CRAFT SERIES

FABULOUS FOLK ART GIFTS

For under $20

JUDY ALLEN & DEBORAH KNEEN

SALLY MILNER PUBLISHING

This book is dedicated with love to my children, Paul, Donna, Christopher and Julie, and to my husband, Tom, and daughter-in-law, Shane.

JUDY ALLEN

First published in 1995 by
Sally Milner Publishing Pty Ltd
558 Darling Street
Rozelle NSW 2039
Australia

© Judy Allen & Deborah Kneen 1995.

Photography by Andrew Elton
Styling by Deborah Kneen and Judy Allen
Illustrations and patterns: copyright Deborah Kneen and Judy Allen, 1995.
Colour separation by Sphere Color Graphics in Brisbane
Printed in Australia by Impact Printing

National Library of Australia
Cataloguing-in-Publication data:

Allen, Judy, 1947 Aug. 15 -
    Fabulous folk art gifts

    ISBN 1 86351 169 5.

    1. Handicraft - Handbooks, manuals, etc. 2. Folk art -
    Handbooks, manuals, etc. 3. Painting - Technique.
    I. Kneen, Deborah. II. Title. (Series : Milner craft series).

745.

CONTENTS

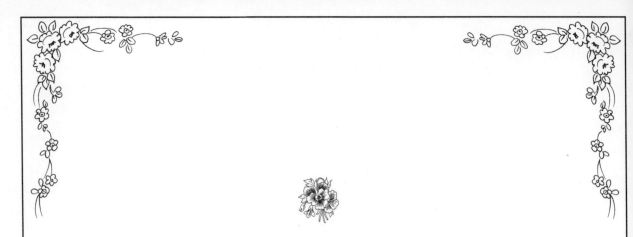

ACKNOWLEDGEMENTS

We are indebted to the following individuals and companies for their assistance: Alderson's Craftmart at Kogarah for fabrics and other props; Jennifer Bowe who generously lent her superb collection of miniature bears for photography, and Denise Lawler. Thanks also to Sue Aiken and Robyn Wilson, and the team at Sally Milner Publishing. Lastly, thanks go to Andrew Elton for his delightful photographs.

From Judy Allen:

Very special thanks and love to my parents, Therese and John. Also to my brothers, Terry and Graham, and their families for their constant praise and support.

Thanks to Elizabeth Roberts for being a lovely friend and sharing in some humble beginnings at Primrose Cottage.

Thank you to all my friends at Alderson's, Lugarno Craft Cottage and Kogarah Bay, and to those special friends and family members who have treasured the gifts I have painted for them.

Heartfelt thanks to my special friend, Deborah, for having faith in my ability to produce this book. Without Deborah's guidance and professionalism, this wonderful experience would not have been possible for me.

From Deborah Kneen:

Special thanks to my co-author, Judy, a wonderful friend and talented artist whose painted gifts were the inspiration behind this book.

A big thank you also to Peter and Brenton who coped patiently with a distracted wife and mother during the gestation period of this book. They would no doubt agree with Gauguin's comment that 'many excellent cooks are spoiled by going into the arts'. And to my lovely mum, Phyll, who is a constant and invaluable source of encouragement as well as practical help and advice.

DISCLAIMER

INTRODUCTION

A gift is as a precious stone in the eyes of him that hath it.

PROVERBS 17: 8

Folk art is the ideal craft for creating inexpensive yet beautiful gifts. All you need is a set of paints and a few brushes, and you can transform everyday items into works of art. This book shows you how to take ready-made objects, available cheaply from discount stores, and decorate them with painted motifs to create unique gifts that will be treasured by their recipients. Not only will you save money, but you will have the satisfaction of creating a gift with your own hands.

We hope that the projects and ideas in this book will encourage you to see the gift potential in even the plainest item. The humble white handkerchief, for example, can be transformed in minutes by adding a painted bouquet. A pair of wine glasses or champagne flutes, when handpainted, become an heirloom wedding or anniversary gift. Through the magic of folk art, small items such as hairclips and headbands can be turned into pretty presents. An ordinary white china cup and saucer set painted with a bouquet of flowers becomes an exquisite piece of heirloom porcelain. There is no limit to the possibilities.

Apart from wood, which has long been the traditional folk art surface, we have also included china, plastic, leather, fabric and glass projects. The recent introduction of non-toxic acrylic enamels and tile and glass mediums has made working with acrylics on slick surfaces like glass and glazed ceramics cheap, successful and safe.

Many of the projects in this book are gifts we have created for our own families and friends over the years. Some pieces are presents we have painted for each other. Our philosophy is to give rather than sell our work.

Giving and receiving folk art gifts is one of the nicest ways of keeping friendship alive. Happy painting!

Judy and Deborah

CHAPTER 1

HOW TO USE THIS BOOK

Browse through the book and decide which project/s you would like to paint. The paint brush code system indicates the level of difficulty.

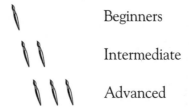

Beginners

Intermediate

Advanced

Once you have chosen a gift, always refer first to the *Useful Information* section (page 3). Read the relevant instructions on preparation, transferring the pattern, painting and finishing the item. In many cases, finishing may include heat-setting.

You should also read the *Paints* section (page 3) to familiarise yourself with the various types of paint used in this book and the best kind of paint for the surface you have chosen. Because of the vast array of paints on the market, we have tried to simplify this for you as much as possible. Where a colour without a brand name appears in the instructions, the paint used is Jo Sonja's Artists' Colours.

The actual instructions for each project are quite brief as many projects share common techniques and these are explained in detail in the *Useful Information* section and illustrated step-by-step in the colour worksheets on pages 70 and 71. Take the example of fabric painting – whether you paint on clothes, handkerchief or cushion covers, the techniques are basically the same.

ADAPTING THE DESIGNS

The designs we have created for you are adaptable to a range of surfaces beyond what we have included in this book. If the pattern is the wrong size for your item, make a hand tracing and reduce or enlarge it on a photocopier. This can be done by small increments until you achieve the appropriate size.

It would also be fun to experiment with colour variations. We tend to use 'pretty' colours but you might like to try bolder combinations.

CHAPTER 2

USEFUL INFORMATION

MATERIALS

ITEMS TO PAINT

This is the fun part of creating folk art gifts. You can find things to paint almost everywhere. If, like us, you love shopping, you will be in your element scouring the shelves of chain and discount stores for objects that can be transformed into special gifts.

Over 50 projects are shown in this book, but they are just the tip of the iceberg. We are discovering new painting surfaces every day: white glazed dinnerware, glasses, glass ornaments, bottles and jars, leather, terracotta, plastic, resin, canvas, fabric, tin, children's toys, ceramic tiles, jewellery – just about any surface can now be painted successfully with specialist acrylics. The new environmentally-aware paint technology has brought us a range of non-toxic paints, suited to all our needs (see *Paints* below and *Surface Preparation* page 6).

PAINTS

Today, decorative painters and hobbyists have access to a huge range of paints. Indeed, the choice is sometimes daunting! We believe the key factor in your choice of paint should be whether it is certified non-toxic. For the sake of your health, avoid oil and solvent-based products, including turpentine. All the paints listed for our projects are water-based, non-aerosol and non-toxic. They all clean up with water.

If you are already a folk artist, you can save money by using your existing paints. For example, Jo Sonja's Artists' Colours can be converted into fabric, glazed ceramic or glass paint, simply by adding the appropriate medium. You can make fabric paint by adding an equal part of Jo Sonja's Textile Medium to Jo Sonja's paints. When the design is dry, it can be heat-set with an iron to make it permanent (see page 16). Similarly, ceramic and glass paint can be made by adding Jo Sonja's Tile and Glass Painting Medium (see pages 15 and 17).

Some other paint brands also offer mediums to convert artists' paints for use on other surfaces. For instance, Plaid FolkArt has a Textile Medium to be used with FolkArt paints. DecoArt also has a Fabric Painting Medium for use with DecoArt Americana acrylics. Try to use the same brand for both medium and paint. Otherwise, there could be a chemical incompatibility between the products. And check the label – each brand has a different mixing ratio:

some are equal parts medium and paint; others are 1 part medium to 2 parts paint, and so on.

You can also buy ready-mixed paints specifically designed for use on shiny surfaces (glass, ceramic, plastic, etc). Examples of these include DecoArt Ultra Gloss, Liquitex Glossies and Matisse Derivan Paint-a-Matazz. These products are acrylic enamels and are certified non-toxic. They give a superb gloss finish and they clean up with water. Colours can be intermixed to give just the right shade. Durability is excellent, but obviously not as strong as kiln-fired glazes.

We recommend that you use these products for *decorative purposes* and do not apply them to any surface that will come into contact with food, drink or lips. Care for your handpainted items by handwashing them. DecoArt Ultra Gloss and Liquitex Glossies can be heat-set for extra durability, but bear in mind the warnings regarding oven fumes on page 17. Items which cannot be placed in an oven can be heat-set with a hairdryer or in the sun.

If you want to paint on fabric, you can use the textile medium method described above, or you can experiment with the many excellent specialist fabric paints on the market. The DecoArt fabric paint range, for example, requires no heat-setting and includes metallic, glitter, sequin, pearlescent, fluorescent and dimensional paints in a brilliant array of colours. See page 14.

Please note that you should always allow the paint (whether it be normal acrylic or specialist paint) to cure, preferably for a week or so, before handling or washing. This means planning ahead with your painting to allow adequate curing time before the gift is wrapped and presented. Although we have been known to paint and heat-set champagne flutes on the morning of the wedding, we do not recommend this practice, except in an emergency.

BRUSHES

You do not need to buy a lot of fancy brushes, particularly if you are just beginning this hobby. There are two main types of brush:

◆ a round brush that has a rounded metal ferrule and a pointed tip on the bristles.

◆ a flat brush that has a flat metal ferrule and squared-off bristles.

Our favourite brushes include a small round brush (No. 2) for general painting purposes, a liner brush for fine details and a selection of flat brushes (say, a No. 2, 4 and 6) for Judy's floated flowers and for shading and highlighting. You will also need a couple of cheap synthetic bristle brushes (2-2.5 cm or ½-¾") for base coating and varnishing.

EXTRAS

Depending on the surface you are painting, you may also need the following:

◆ Sea or synthetic sponge for sponged background effects.

◆ Tracing paper to trace patterns.

◆ Graphite pencil.

◆ Chalk pencil.

◆ One sheet each of grey graphite and white transfer paper.

◆ Fabric transfer pen (optional).

◆ Empty biro or stylus for transferring patterns.

◆ Scotch Transparent Magic Tape for holding patterns in place whilst transferring them.

◆ Piece of strong cardboard covered in plastic food wrap (for painting T-shirts, etc).

◆ Non-stick baking paper to use as palette paper.

◆ Ruler.

◆ Eraser.

◆ Cotton buds for removing 'mistakes'. For wet paint, dampen the cotton bud with water. For stubborn, dry paint, use nail polish remover.

◆ Sandpaper.

◆ Soft, absorbent rags.

◆ Water jar or brush basin.

◆ Tiles or plastic plates to use as blending surfaces for flat brush work.

◆ Hand soap for cleaning brushes.

◆ Sealer and water-based matte or satin varnish.

SURFACE PREPARATION

Surface preparation can often be tedious, but a well-prepared surface may mean the difference between success and disaster in terms of the finished gift. After all, if you are painting a present for someone, you want it to last. Imagine how you would feel if the paint cracked, bubbled or peeled off on the present you had given a friend.

WOOD

Preparation of wood will depend upon the type of wood and condition of the surface.

MEDIUM DENSITY FIBREBOARD

Take great care when sanding medium density fibreboard (Craftwood). It produces dangerous fibres and fumes. We always seal it first and try to avoid sanding. If you **must** sand, wear a mask and work outside. Rough or furry routed edges can be concealed with several coats of gesso.

RAW WOOD

If the wood is rough, sand well in the direction of the grain and wipe clean. You are now ready to basecoat, stain, pickle or whatever. If you have a nice piece of wood, you can seal it with Jo Sonja's All Purpose Sealer and paint your design directly onto the plain wood.

STAINED WOOD

We have had great success painting on pre-stained wood. The main prerequisite is to create a bond between the slightly shiny stained surface and the paint. To do this, we scuff up the area where the design will go with a kitchen scourer or fine sandpaper to create a 'key' to which the paint can adhere.

METAL

Ensure the surface is clean and rust-free. New metal should be washed with a solution of vinegar and water, then dried thoroughly. If you intend to expose the finished article to the elements, metal should initially be sealed with metal primer. Then basecoat in the colour of your choice. We find proprietary basecoats, made by companies such as Plaid FolkArt, DecoArt and Jo Sonja, and available in 250 ml bottles, are ideal for this. Finish with polyurethane varnish.

FABRIC

Wash and dry the fabric but do not use fabric softener. Press the item before transferring the pattern. Before painting, place a plastic-covered sheet of cardboard, cut to the appropriate size, inside cushion and pillow covers, lingerie bags, T-shirts and sweatshirts to hold the fabric taut and prevent paint seeping through to the back of the item or garment.

TERRACOTTA

We have seen painters work on terracotta without any surface preparation but we feel it is best to hose down or wash the terracotta to remove salts. Then while semi-wet, seal the surface with Jo Sonja's All Purpose Sealer (don't use too much!). Because terracotta is so porous, the sealer seems to go on better when the surface is damp rather than dry. A sponge-brush (i.e. a handle with a square sponge at the end) works well on terracotta, or you can use a synthetic basecoating brush. Never use good brushes to seal terracotta.

CANVAS

Canvas items (hats, espadrilles, director's chair covers, beach umbrellas, tote bags) can be painted without any preparation. Never pre-wash these articles or they will lose their sizing and become limp.

If you are painting canvas shoes or hats, stuff the item with paper towel or tissue paper covered in plastic food wrap.

Use the same paints you would use for fabric, preferably those that do not require heat-setting.

GLASS

Take a mixture of vinegar and water (about 20 percent vinegar) and wipe the glass clean. Rinse off the vinegar and water solution and dry the glass. Do not use commercial glass cleaners as they may leave behind a film on the surface which prevents the paint adhering to the surface. Use acrylic enamels or artists' acrylics with the appropriate medium (see pages 3 and 4).

PLASTIC AND LEATHER

Ensure the surface is clean and dry. Use acrylic enamels.

GLAZED CERAMIC

Wipe the surface clean as described above under **Glass**. No other preparation is necessary when decorating with acrylic enamels or artists' acrylics with the appropriate medium (see pages 3 and 4).

BISQUE PORCELAIN

Bisque is porcelain that has been fired to maximum strength but is unglazed. It has a white, matte appearance. Ensure the surface is smooth and free of dust. Sand any ridges carefully with a kitchen scourer. Remove dust with a small paintbrush.

Bisque will need to be sealed because it is very porous. Then basecoat with artists' acrylic paint. When dry, you can then paint your design with the same acrylic paints.

If a gloss finish is desired, allow your painting to dry, then varnish with a water-based gloss varnish.

CANDLES

If you are in a hurry, you can paint directly onto the candle with ordinary artists' acrylics. Ideally, however, you should seal the general area you plan to decorate and a little beyond with Jo Sonja's All Purpose Sealer. There is no need to seal the entire candle. Allow the sealer to dry overnight, then repeat. When the second coat of sealer is thoroughly dry, paint your design. We work freehand on candles – it is almost impossible to transfer a pattern, particularly on narrow candles. Allow the paint to dry well. Then varnish the design area with your favourite water-based varnish. Another method is to use acrylic enamels directly on the candles – no initial sealer and no finishing varnish. Do not heat-set.

A tip for those using the sealer, acrylic paint and varnish method: Before wrapping the candle, ensure the varnished design is completely dry. In addition, always wrap the candle loosely. We have had a disaster where we wrapped a gift to find the whole painted design had peeled off the candle and adhered to the cellophane wrap!

TRANSFERRING PATTERNS

Trace the appropriate pattern from this book onto tracing paper. If it is the wrong size, it can be reduced or enlarged on a photocopier. See also the note on page 19.

HARD SURFACES

For hard surfaces such as wood, bisque and tin (not glass), use transfer paper available from art and craft suppliers.

Trace the pattern onto tracing paper, then align on your surface and secure with Scotch Magic Tape. Slip a sheet of transfer paper underneath. Use grey graphite for light base colours and white for dark backgrounds. Coloured transfer papers (blue, yellow, etc) tend to contain wax and are difficult to erase.

Ensure that the transfer paper is placed with the graphite side towards the surface. Now trace lightly over the pattern with an empty ballpoint pen or a stylus. For designs involving transparent techniques, use a very light touch or the pattern lines will show through. Do not transfer fine details which will be painted over anyway. If necessary, these can be transferred after the main elements have been blocked in.

Transfer paper can be used over and over again. Indeed, the older the sheet, the less chance of it producing unwanted smudges on your work.

When you have finished painting, always erase any pattern lines that may still be showing *before* varnishing.

FABRIC

One of the easiest ways to transfer a pattern onto semi-transparent surfaces such as light-coloured fabric is to use a light box or a well-lit window. Tape the pattern (right side facing you) onto the glass, then place the fabric or paper over it so that the pattern is correctly positioned. Secure the fabric with Scotch Magic Tape. Lightly trace over the design with a pencil.

You can make your own light box with a piece of glass resting on a couple of telephone books with a lamp placed underneath the glass. Our friend Joyce Spencer suggests padding the corners of the glass with masking tape to avoid accidents.

If the fabric is thick and/or dark coloured, you may have difficulty seeing through it. In these cases, use the appropriately coloured transfer paper and follow the methods described in *Hard Surfaces* or use a transfer pen (see below).

For a heavy sweatshirt, pattern transfer will be easier if you stretch the fabric taut by placing an appropriately sized sheet of heavy cardboard inside the shirt. Then secure the pattern with Scotch Magic Tape or pins. Transfer the design with a stylus and transfer paper.

Alternately, a commercial transfer pen can be used. Simply trace the pattern onto tracing paper with a felt pen. Then trace over the reverse side of the pattern lines with the transfer pen. Place the pattern right side up on the fabric in the appropriate place and secure with pins. Iron over it with a warm iron to transfer the design. Check under an edge to ensure the pattern is transferring.

GLASS

For a glass surface, position and secure the pattern behind the glass with Scotch Magic Tape. You can then paint directly from the pattern. You can also sketch on your design with a marking pen.

PAINTING TERMS AND TECHNIQUES

Here are some tips for avoiding pitfalls and problems and creating a successful painted gift.

GENERAL PAINTING TIPS FOR ALL SURFACES

BRUSH-MIXING

Instead of mixing the paint thoroughly with a palette knife, brush-mixing involves picking up the various colours on your brush and blending them together casually on the palette before making a stroke. A cooking analogy would be lightly folding in ingredients, as opposed to beating them all together. Brush-mixing tends to give your work more character because the individual colours, though not distinct in the finished stroke, have not been mixed to the point of disappearing. Doubleloading takes this process one step further by having two distinct colours on the brush and in the finished stroke.

COMMA STROKES

Comma strokes are the basis of folk art. Although they can be painted with a flat brush, we like to use a No. 2 or 3 round brush. Dip the brush into a fresh pile of paint, then start at the fattest part of the comma and press down on the bristles. Pull the stroke down and lift to form a sharp point.

DIMENSIONAL PAINT

We talk about the use of dimensional paint on fabric on page 14, but you should also be aware that it works brilliantly on other surfaces such as paper and wood. Remember to shake the bottle well and practise on paper first to acquire a feel for the pressure required for dots, strokes and lines. Mistakes can be removed while the paint is wet by using a damp cotton bud, but it is an awkward process. Dimensional paint can also be brushed on if you need to touch up untidy areas.

DOUBLELOADING A FLAT BRUSH

To double load is to carry two colours, often two values of the same colour, on the brush at the same time. With a flat brush, load one corner with the lighter value colour and dip the other corner into the darker value colour. Be generous with the paint when loading and ensure the paint consistency is creamy. Add retarder to the brush, if necessary. Blend well in the one spot on your palette until the two colours merge in the centre of the brush. Then make your stroke and, hey presto, you have an instant gradation of colour.

DOUBLELOADING A ROUND BRUSH

You need to be able to carry two distinct colours on your brush at the one time. Experiment with different methods of loading the round brush to obtain different results. For example, loading the two colours beside each other will create a different stroke from stroking the front of the brush across one colour and the back of the brush across another. You can also load fully into one colour and tip into the other.

FLOATED COLOUR

To float colour, you will need a good-quality flat brush. Its size will depend on the area to be covered, but, for general purposes, use a No. 6, 8 or 10 flat. The larger the area, the bigger the brush. First, dip the brush into water, retarder or Clear Medium (for Ultra Gloss) and blot slightly on a soft, absorbent rag. Then corner in the colour of your choice. Blend on your palette until the paint has spread about two-thirds of the way across the brush with a gradation of colour from intense to very watery to

nothing. You may need to reload your brush and repeat if you were too sparing with the paint the first time.

Now make your stroke, pressing down evenly and firmly on the bristles. Remember to face the corner of the brush with the paint on it towards the area that is to be darkest. If your floating looks like a harsh outline rather than graduated shading, it is probably caused by one of the following:

◆ You did not load enough paint initially.

◆ Your brush was too small – try a larger size.

◆ You did not blend sufficiently on your palette – this is all-important. Press down and make the bristles of your brush flare out.

◆ You were working up on the corner of the brush when you made the stroke rather than applying equal pressure across the bristles.

Tips for successful floating

If you still can't get it right, try this hint. Load your brush first in the base colour (right across the bristles), then corner into the floating colour. Now blend on your palette and make the stroke. You will find the effect is much softer. Another excellent tip is to pre-wet the area to be floated with water or retarder, then float. The float will not 'grab' the surface.

Avoid narrow floated shadows that look like outlines. If this happens to you, allow the float to dry, then apply a second float starting just inside the edge of the first. When applying floats, try to 'walk' the colour outwards to give a broader shadow. If a float has dried and you feel it is too dark, float over it with your original base colour.

LINER WORK

For fine, detailed work you need a good-quality liner brush. We favour a script liner, a brush with extra-long bristles, because we can load a lot of paint onto it and paint longer, flowing lines without having to reload. Apart from a good brush, paint consistency is the key to proficient liner work – paint must be watered down to an inky consistency. You will need to thin tube acrylic significantly more than bottle acrylic. Use water, not retarder, to thin the paint for liner work. Roll the brush in the paint so that it forms a point. Take care that you do not have a blob of paint on the end of your brush – this will result in thick or uneven lines. You need to experiment to find just the right consistency that flows well, does not drag and is not too runny.

SIDELOADING

To sideload is to take paint only onto one corner of the brush. You can sideload both a round and a flat brush. After sideloading a flat brush, blend well on your palette to remove excess paint and to create a gradation of colour. See also **Floated Colour** above.

PAINTING TIPS FOR FABRIC

◆ When mixing up your own fabric paints by using artists' acrylics plus textile or fabric medium, follow the manufacturer's mixing instructions carefully. Use egg cartons or icecube trays to mix and store each colour. If you have to stop painting for some reason, seal the container with plastic food wrap to keep the paint fresh.

◆ When painting on cushion and pillow covers, linen lingerie bags, T-shirts and sweatshirts, you need to prevent paint seeping through to the back of the article. Cut a piece of cardboard to the appropriate size and cover it with plastic food wrap. Place inside the item. The cardboard will also hold it taut to make painting easier. You can also secure the item to the board with pins or masking tape.

◆ For a very large item, such as a man's sweatshirt or a tablecloth, Judy suggests placing a piece of plastic-covered cardboard a little bigger than the design inside the shirt or underneath the cloth and then wrapping up the excess fabric like a parcel and securing it at the back with masking tape or pins. Not only will this make painting easier, but it will prevent the excess fabric from being accidentally smudged with paint.

◆ Always keep your work area and your hands scrupulously clean when working with fabric.

◆ If you do smudge your work, try to remove the stain with a damp cotton bud. If unsuccessful, try a cotton bud dipped in nail polish remover, but do not use on delicate fabrics and test first in an unobtrusive place to ensure the nail polish remover will not harm the fabric. If the smudge is stubborn, you can always incorporate it into the design by making it a leaf, tendril or swirl.

◆ Washes on fabric are difficult to control, owing to the porous nature of the surface. If you want to create soft areas of transparent colour such as the background on the Teddy T-shirt (page 74), do not add large amounts of water to the paint. This will result in uncontrolled bleeding and blooming of the paint. Instead, pre-wet the area to be washed with thickener (such as Plaid FolkArt Thickener), then water down the paint just a little or dilute it with extra thickener. The thickener will help to control the wash and keep the colour transparent. Thickener evaporates on drying.

◆ When working on a dark-coloured background, base your flowers and leaves in a light, neutral colour, such as Smoked Pearl and allow to dry. Judy also recommends basecoating teddy bears in the same colour. Because fabric is so absorbent and tends to soak up a lot of paint, this will help to give good coverage and prevent the background colour showing through.

◆ Do not mix standard artists' acrylics with ready-mixed fabric paints. This will lessen the bonding power of the paint.

◆ Glitter fabric paints require two heavy coats, with the second coat applied within an hour of the first.

◆ When using textured paints such as glitters and dimensionals, wipe brushes regularly on a paper towel and clean with hand soap to avoid build-up of paint residue in the ferrule (metal part of the brush).

◆ Dimensional paints tend to clog so, before use, turn the bottle upside down (with the lid on) and tap well to remove air bubbles. Clogged tips can be cleared with a pin or piece of wire. Always test a dimensional on a scrap of paper before using it on the actual surface.

◆ When using dimensional paints over ready-mixed fabric paints, allow the paint to dry for an hour or two before applying the dimensional paint. If the underlying colour is too wet, the dimensional paint will tend to flatten out.

◆ Dimensional paint cannot be used over certain metallics (DecoArt Dazzling Metallics are an example) as it will not adhere properly. Check the manufacturer's instructions. You can, however, use the dimensional paint *next to* the Dazzling Metallics paint if the dimensional is applied directly to the fabric.

PAINTING TIPS FOR SHINY SURFACES

◆ When using ready-mixed acrylic enamels such as DecoArt Ultra Gloss and Liquitex Glossies, shake the container well before use. You can mix the colours together to achieve other colours. As their names suggest, these paints dry with a gloss finish.

◆ When using Jo Sonja's Glass and Tile Painting Medium, mix 3 parts medium with 1 part Jo Sonja's Artists' Colours. This medium gives the finished painting a matte finish. After heat-setting (page 17), you may wish to apply a coat of Jo Sonja's Water Based Gloss Polyurethane Varnish for a glossy look.

◆ Do **not** paint areas that will come into contact with food, drink or lips.

◆ Never thin acrylic enamel paints with water. This will weaken their strength and lessen adhesion to the surface. The paints are best used straight from the container. Even water left in brushes after washing can affect paint adhesion so dry your brush on a cloth each time you wash it. DecoArt Ultra Gloss can be thinned successfully with DecoArt Clear Medium to create washes and transparent effects.

◆ When applying multiple coats, allow about one hour drying time between coats. This also applies if you want to add floated shading or highlights. If you try to apply a second coat while the first is tacky, the paint will lift.

◆ DecoArt's Ultra Gloss Glitters create interesting effects but require two or three coats with about one hour's drying time between each coat.

◆ DecoArt make a metal tip called the Deco Fine Liner, which is excellent for fine lines and lettering. It is ideal for writing a special name or initials on glass or china. You can use it successfully with Ultra Gloss Acrylics and Metallics, but not with Ultra Gloss Glitters as they will clog the tip.

◆ Wash out brushes immediately after use with hand soap and water.

◆ Dimensional paints work well on shiny surfaces. Experiment with them as accents and for textured effects.

◆ For heat-setting details, see page 17.

Specific Hints for Glass Painting

◆ If you are used to painting on wood, you will need to take into account that glass is transparent, and consequently paint coverage will not be as good. For a more opaque effect, you will need to apply several coats. Wait until the first coat is dry before applying the next.

◆ You will find it easier to see what you are doing, if you place a white tissue inside the glass while painting.

Finishing, Heat-setting and Maintenance

WOOD

◆ We like to finish a wooden item with a couple of coats of water-based matte or satin varnish. This enhances the colours and also protects the surface. If you have painted the design on a commercially stained surface, varnish only the design area, not the whole item, as the varnish may be incompatible with the original stain, particularly if it is oil-based.

◆ If you are unfamiliar with a particular varnish, always test it first on an unobtrusive part of the item, such as the bottom of a box or tray. If there is a problem, the area can be sanded off without damaging your masterpiece.

FABRIC

◆ Always read the manufacturer's instructions carefully. Most modern ready-mixed fabric paints, including glitters, iridescents and metallics, do not require heat-setting, but some of the earlier brands on the market do need to be heat-set. Where specified, heat-setting ensures that colours won't run or fade after washing.

◆ If you make your own fabric paint by adding fabric medium, you will need to heat-set the finished design. First, ensure the paint is dry – fabric paints take longer than standard acrylics. Also remember to remove the cardboard backing before heat-setting. Place a tea-towel or piece of brown paper over the painted area and press with a warm iron (not steam setting) for a couple of minutes. You can also repeat the same process on the reverse of the design. On fiddly items, such as canvas hats and shoes, use a hairdryer for a couple of minutes.

◆ If you have made your own fabric paints with fabric medium and want to add dimensional accents, do this after heat-setting, otherwise you will flatten the dimensional paint. Dimensionals do not need to be heat-set.

◆ We recommend handwashing painted garments and other items such as pillow covers – after all, they are works of art and should be cared for accordingly. Always wait a week or so after painting before washing. Avoid washing detergents with bleach, chlorine or other whitening agents. Lay the garment flat and air dry away from the sun – do not use a clothes dryer. Why not include a little card with your gift saying: *Please gently handwash and air dry away from the sun.*

GLASS AND GLAZED CERAMICS

◆ If you use the acrylic enamel paints such as DecoArt Ultra Gloss, Liquitex Glossies or Matisse Derivan Paint-a-Matazz, they become extremely durable after a week or two of curing time and do not have to be heat-set. But please note that they are not as durable as kiln-fired glazes.

◆ The manufacturers of DecoArt Ultra Gloss and Liquitex Glossies suggest that, for dishwasher durability, 'oven-safe' items can be heat-set in a home oven (not a microwave). You need to let the article cure for 24 hours before heat-setting. Then place it in a cold oven and set at the temperature specified on the label. When the correct temperature is reached, bake for 30 minutes (ready-mixed paints) or 45 minutes (glass and tile medium). Owners of fan-forced ovens may need to lower temperatures a little (by about 10 degrees Celsius). Let the oven cool completely before removing the item.

NOTE: We think that, as these items are 'works of art', they should be handwashed and, therefore, dishwasher safety is not an issue.

◆ If you insist on heat-setting, do not bake at higher temperatures than those indicated or excessive fumes will result. If you plan to undertake this process regularly, we suggest you purchase a small oven to use exclusively for this purpose and keep it in a well-ventilated studio – not your kitchen. If you do heat-set in the same oven you use for baking food (and we

do not recommend this), we suggest airing the oven to remove any remaining fumes before using it for baking food. In addition, you should run the exhaust fan in your kitchen during and after heat-setting

◆ Some items may be too large for the oven or they may be unsuitable for baking. They can be heat-set with a hairdryer – on low and not placed too close. Appropriate items can also be placed in the sun to harden the paint.

◆ Remember that if you have used Jo Sonja's Tile and Glass Painting Medium and you want a shiny finish to your design, you will need to varnish the design with Jo Sonja's Water Based Gloss Polyurethane Varnish (after heat-setting).

◆ The manufacturers tell us that the acrylic enamel paints are dishwasher-safe after baking in the oven. Nevertheless, to be on the safe side, we again recommend handwashing. If you or the gift's recipient do place the item in the dishwasher, you should be aware that the heat of the dishwasher can cause the paint to become 'tender' temporarily. So you must be very careful until the item cools and the paint hardens again.

◆ And remember our safety warning. These paints should not be used on any surface that will come into contact with lips, food or beverages. And take care with fumes when heat-setting in an oven.

PLASTIC AND LEATHER

◆ Painted designs on plastic and leather (such as wallets, coin purses, diaries, sunglasses, etc) cannot, for obvious reasons, be baked in the oven. If you have used Liquitex Glossies, DecoArt Ultra Gloss or Matisse Derivan Paint-a-Matazz, this is not necessary. If desired, you can use the hairdryer method described above, to harden the paint. But remember, not too hot and not too close!

CHAPTER 3

GIFTS TO WEAR AND CARRY

Handpainted clothes make wonderful gifts. The racks of your local chain store are filled with plain T-shirts, sweatshirts, canvas hats and other items, just waiting to be transformed into one-off designer garments through the magic of folk art. You could even paint matching canvas sneakers or espadrilles. Canvas handbags and totebags are also excellent painting surfaces.

For less expensive wearable gifts, look at hairclips, barrettes and headbands. These are great when you need multiple gifts at Christmas for your children's friends, and they can be painted in minutes.

Most of the patterns throughout this book are 100%. To enlarge the patterns that have been reduced, use a photocopier and key in the percentages given.

\ \ \ HANKY (JUDY) (PHOTO PAGE 21)

Judy has been painting hankies as gifts for many years. They are amongst the quickest and cheapest folk art gifts.

Paints: Indian Red Oxide, Matisse Antique Green, Warm White, Smoked Pearl. Add Textile Medium.

Brushes: No. 4 flat, No. 2 round.

Preparation: Read the section on fabric preparation (page 7).

Roses: Mix a small amount of Indian Red Oxide into Smoked Pearl to give a medium value colour for one rose. Add more Smoked Pearl for the lighter rose. Paint the roses as for the Pillowcase, page 57.

Hanky pattern 100%

Buds: Using the No. 2 round brush, load with the rose colour and sideload with Warm White. Press the brush down and lift up to a point. Using whatever paint is on your brush, add tiny dots here and there to bring the pattern together.

Leaves: Using a No. 2 round, load into Antique Green and sideload into Warm White. The leaves towards the edges of the pattern are less distinct. Paint them softly with only a small amount of paint on your brush.

Pattern 100%
Variation

MELANIE'S HEADBAND (DEBORAH)
(PHOTO PAGE 21)

Paints: Rose Pink, Warm White, Pine Green, Turner's Yellow. Add Textile Medium to the preceding colours.

Brushes: No. 2 round brush.

Extras: Dimensional paint in white pearlescent colour. See hints for using dimensional paint on page 11.

Preparation: None. Paint directly onto the headband. We suggest working freehand, using the photograph as a reference. The flowers are the same as those on the plastic hairclip (page 29) but are placed in a line. Ensure the flowers become smaller as they graduate out from the centre.

Roses: Doubleloaded Rose Pink and Warm White.

Leaves: Doubleloaded Pine Green and Warm White.

Daisies: Warm White petals. Turner's Yellow centres.

Add dimensional dots in pearlescent white as accents. They give the flowers an embroidered look.

Finishing: No finishing is required for ready-mixed fabric paints. To increase durability of acrylics plus fabric medium, heat-set with a hairdryer.

Headband pattern 100%

SHELL T-SHIRT AND SUNSHADE (PAGE 32)

CHRISTMAS T-SHIRT (PAGE 34) CHRISTMAS GLASS (PAGE 48)

CUTWORK PILLOW (PAGE 59) FLORAL T-SHIRT (PAGE 30)
AND CANVAS HATBOX (PAGE 25)

CANVAS HATBOX (DEBORAH)
(PHOTO PAGE 24)

Deborah was given this (unpainted) canvas hatbox by her friend, Bernadette, who suggested she might like to decorate it. This lavish Second Empire floral design, inspired by an antique French tapestry, is the result. If you can't find a similar canvas hat box, paint the design on a black canvas handbag or totebag. The canvas background makes the flowers look embroidered rather than painted. Because Deborah wanted to maintain the textured tapestry look on the canvas, she did not add Textile Medium to the paint. Anyway, Textile Medium is not necessary for this project as the hatbox will not be washed, and the paint adheres well to the canvas surface without Textile Medium.

Paints: Warm White, Yellow Oxide, Napthol Crimson, Red Earth, Indian Red Oxide, Brown Earth, Pine Green. Plaid FolkArt Summer Sky (a light grey-blue).

Brushes: No. 2 round brush, No. 6 flat brush for floated shading.

Preparation: No preparation.

General tips: All painting, except floated shading, is done with a No. 2 round brush. The flowers are very relaxed and casual, so the painter should be the same. A tense hand will produce rigid-looking flowers, so relax that wrist and take lots of deep breaths.

Hatbox pattern
Enlarge at 140%

The paint is blended wet-in-wet, so be generous when loading your brush.

Pink rose: Paint a section at a time, using a generous doubleload of Napthol Crimson and Warm White. While wet, add some Warm White highlights to the bowl and tips of the petals. Shade the dark areas (see photo) with the base colour plus Indian Red Oxide. The throat is Indian Red Oxide.

Yellow rose: The yellow rose is doubleloaded Yellow Oxide and Warm White. The throat is Brown Earth.

Burgundy rose: Doubleloaded Indian Red Oxide and Warm White. The centre is Pine Green plus Warm White.

Large open flower: Tripleloaded Warm White, Yellow Oxide and Raw Sienna. Follow the shape of each petal. Overstroke with extra Warm White. Deepen the area around the centre with Indian Red Oxide. The centre is a dot of doubleloaded Pine Green and Warm White.

Yellow daisies: Doubleloaded Warm White and Yellow Oxide. Shade around centres with Indian Red Oxide. Centres are Warm White with a little Yellow Oxide. Add a dot of Pine Green or Indian Red Oxide.

Pink carnation (on right): Doubleloaded Indian Red Oxide and Warm White. Calyx is Pine Green plus Warm White.

Burgundy buds: Doubleloaded Indian Red Oxide and Warm White. Calyx as for carnation.

Blue flowers: Doubleloaded Summer Sky and Warm White. Centres are Yellow Oxide, outlined with Brown Earth. Paint a Pine Green dot in the very centre.

Rose and open flower leaves: Follow the texture of the leaf, working a vein area at a time. Brush-mixed Pine Green and Warm White, Yellow Oxide and Raw Sienna.

Ribbon leaves: As for the rose leaves.

Stems: Doubleloaded Pine Green and Warm White.

Finishing: Deborah did not finish her hatbox in any way. She has used it constantly, without damage to the design. If you are worried about the painting becoming soiled, you could Scotchgard® it.

\ \ EVENING BAG (JUDY)
(PHOTO ON BACK COVER)

Paints: Red Earth, Smoked Pearl, Rich Gold, Burnt Sienna, Matisse Antique Green. Add Textile Medium to all preceding colours.

Brushes: No. 2 flat brush, No. 4 flat brush, No. 00 liner brush.

Preparation: None.

Leaves: Doubleload a No. 2 flat with Antique Green and Rich Gold. Paint doubleloaded flat brush leaves as shown in the colour guide on page 70.

Float roses: Refer to the colour worksheet on page 70. Doubleload the No. 4 flat with a mixture of Burnt Sienna and Smoked Pearl on one side and Warm White on the other. Paint the petals. Shade the centres with Burnt Sienna. Add tiny Rich Gold dots to the throats with a liner brush.

Dot daisies: Rich Gold. No centres. Add fine outlines of Rich Gold as desired.

Finishing: Use a hairdryer to heat-set this design. Add a tassel to your bag as a finishing touch.

Evening Bag
pattern 100%

Judy · 1994 ·

COIN PURSE (JUDY) (PHOTO PAGE 43)

Paints: Indian Red Oxide, Yellow Oxide, Warm White, Red Earth, Carbon Black, Matisse Antique Green.

Brushes: No. 2 round brush, No. 00 liner brush.

Preparation: No preparation is required.

Leaves: Load a No. 2 round with Antique Green and sideload with Warm White.

Pansies: Add Warm White to Yellow Oxide to form a light yellow. Paint the top petals with two coats of this colour. Shade at the centre with Indian Red Oxide. Side petals are Indian Red Oxide. Shade at the centre with light yellow, using a liner brush. The bottom petal is light yellow, again shaded with Indian Red Oxide. Add a deeper yellow (less Warm White) under the centre. Paint a Red Earth dot in the centre with a Carbon Black and Warm White dot underneath. Paint a comma stroke of Warm White on either side of the centre with a liner brush.

Daisies: With a No. 2 round, paint light yellow petals, a Warm White centre and Indian Red Oxide dots under the centre.

Dot daisies: Paint in Warm White with a liner brush. Add an Indian Red Oxide centre. The side petals are light yellow with a tiny Warm White dot on the end of the stroke.

Finishing: When dry, use a hairdryer to heat-set.

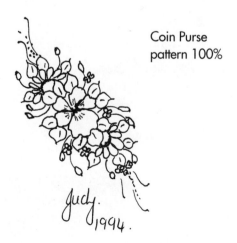

Coin Purse
pattern 100%

❧ PLASTIC HAIRCLIP (DEBORAH)
(PHOTO PAGE 21)

Paints: Rose Pink, Titanium White, Pine Green, Yellow Oxide, Gold Oxide, Brown Earth, Dioxazine Purple, Plaid FolkArt Summer Sky (a light grey-blue). Plus Jo Sonja's Glass and Tile Painting Medium added to each colour (see page 3).

Hairclip pattern 100%

Paint the florals as for the coffee cup on page 38, but remember they are very tiny so keep them simple.

Brushes: No. 2 round brush.

Preparation: None.

Finishing: Harden the painted design by heat-setting with a hairdryer – not too hot!

❧❧ BROOCH (JUDY) (PHOTO ON BACK COVER)

Paints: Indian Red Oxide, Carbon Black, Yellow Oxide, Warm White, Rich Gold.

Brushes: No. 2 round brush, No 0 or 1 round brush, No. 00 liner brush.

Preparation: Basecoat wooden insert with Smoked Pearl. Trace on pattern.

Roses: The roses are painted with a No. 2 flat brush, using the float rose method shown in the colour worksheet on page 70. Use Indian Red Oxide and Warm White.

Leaves and stems: Use a No. 0 or No. 1 round brush, loaded in green mixture (Yellow Oxide plus Carbon Black) and sideloaded in Rich Gold.

Buds: Buds are Indian Red Oxide with tiny Warm White liner work dots.

Brooch pattern 100%

Floated edge: With a No. 2 flat brush, float Indian Red Oxide around the edge to form a soft border.

Finishing: Varnish with three coats of water-based matte or satin varnish. Glue the insert inside the frame.

\ \ FLORAL T-SHIRT (JUDY) (PHOTO PAGE 24)

Floral T-shirt pattern
100% – left shoulder

Judy painted this T-shirt for Deborah's birthday several years ago. It has been worn frequently and handwashed regularly, but as you can see in the photo, it still looks like new. This says a lot for Judy's preparation and the products she used.

Paints: Indian Red Oxide, Yellow Oxide, Smoked Pearl, Warm White, Red Earth, Carbon Black, Rich Gold. Add Textile Medium to all preceding colours. Plus Matisse Gold Glitz-a-Matazz.

Brushes: No. 4 flat brush, No. 4 round brush, No. 00 liner brush.

Preparation: Transfer the pattern as explained on page 9. Remember to place a plastic-wrapped T-shirt board inside (page 13).
Unless otherwise stated, use your No. 4 round brush.

Leaves: Mix a small amount of Carbon Black into Yellow Oxide to make a dark green. Basecoat all leaves with this colour. When dry, load the No. 4 flat brush with dark green and corner into Warm White. Paint flat brush leaves (see colour guide page 70). Every now and then, doubleload with Indian Red Oxide and Warm White.

Roses: Basecoat all roses with Smoked Pearl. When dry, doubleload the No. 4 flat brush with Indian Red Oxide and Warm White. Paint large float roses as shown in colour on page 70. Shade the centres with Indian Red Oxide. With a liner brush, paint small dots of Warm White and Rich Gold respectively in the centres.

Pansies: Basecoat each petal of the pansy with Smoked Pearl. When dry, paint the petals either Yellow Oxide or Indian Red Oxide. When dry, take the No. 4 flat brush and load with the petal colour and sideload with Warm White to create frilly edges.

Filler flowers: Dot daisies are Warm White. Centres are Rich Gold and Yellow Oxide.

Finishing: Heat-set when dry. Add Gold Glitz to decorate, as shown in the colour photograph.

Floral T-shirt pattern
Enlarge at 125%

Judy 92

\\ \\ Shell T-shirt and Sunshade (Judy)
(photo page 22)

Paints: Smoked Pearl, White Pearl, French Blue, Yellow Oxide, Warm White, Carbon Black, Pale Gold. Add Textile Medium to all preceding colours. Matisse Glitz-a-Matazz in Gold.

Brushes: No. 2 round brush, No. 4 round brush.

Preparation: Prepare fabric according to the instructions on page 7. Remember to place a plastic-wrapped T-shirt board inside (page 13).

Fish (T-shirt): Basecoat all fish with Smoked Pearl. Some fish are Yellow Oxide and White Pearl. The other fish are French Blue and White Pearl. Outline the fish with Gold Glitz. The eyes are a Gold Glitz circle with a dot in the centre.

Fish (sunshade): Base with two coats of Pale Gold. Paint the features with a liner brush. The eye is Warm White, outlined with Carbon Black. The mouth is Carbon Black. Outline the fish with Gold Glitz.

Shells: Basecoat the shells with Smoked Pearl. Mix French Blue and White Pearl and paint areas of the shells with this blue colour. The other areas are Pale Gold. Outline the shells and circles with Gold Glitz. Add accents of Gold Glitz.

Finishing: Heat-set the T-shirt by ironing (page 16). Heat-set the sunshade with a hairdryer. Add gold shell or fish charms (available from craft and haberdashery shops) to the T-shirt after heat-setting. Always sign your T-shirt.

Judy made a matching bangle by gluing shells onto a plain wooden bangle and painting the whole thing with Rich Gold.

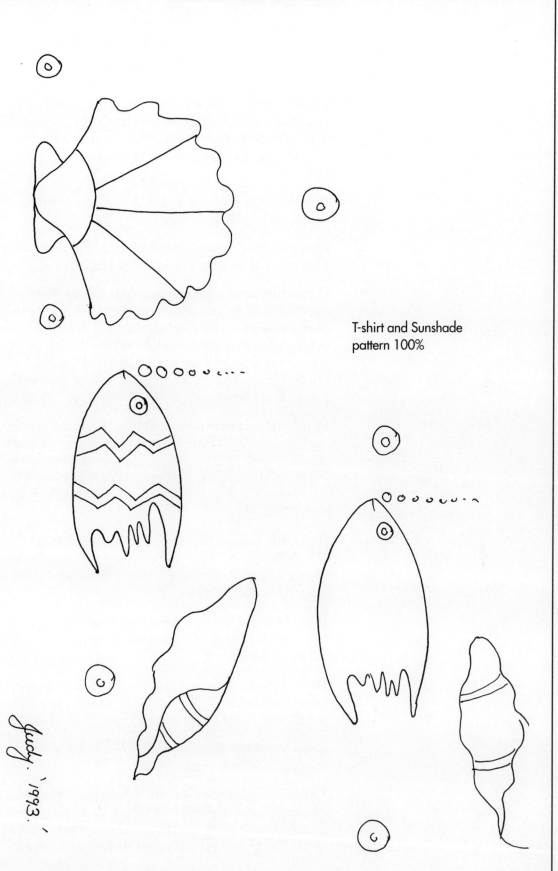

T-shirt and Sunshade
pattern 100%

\ \ \ CHRISTMAS T-SHIRT (JUDY)
(PHOTO PAGE 23)

Paints: Matisse Napthol Scarlet, Jade, Pine Green, Teal Green, Rich Gold, Yellow Oxide, Burnt Sienna, Warm White, Indian Red Oxide. Add Textile Medium to all preceding colours. Matisse Glitz-a-Matazz in Green and Gold.

Brushes: No. 2 round brush, No. 4 round brush, No. 6 flat brush, No. 00 liner brush.

Preparation: Remember to place a plastic-wrapped T-shirt board inside (page 13). Read pages 13 and 14.

Poinsettia petals: Mix a small amount of Yellow Oxide into Napthol Scarlet and paint the petals with two coats of this colour, using the No. 4 round brush. Turn a few petals by adding a sideload of Warm White. To paint a turned petal, start from the tip, press down, pull and lift up. Shade around the centre and tips of the petals with Indian Red Oxide.

Poinsettia centre: Load a No. 4 round brush with medium Green (Pine Green plus Warm White) and sideload with Warm White. Dab on a large amount of paint to the centre. Allow to dry. Add small accent strokes with a liner brush, using Yellow Oxide sideloaded with Warm White.

Poinsettia leaves: Base with Pine Green. Let dry. Using a No. 6 flat brush, load in Pine Green and sideload with Warm White. Paint a few leaves using Pine Green and a sideload of Burnt Sienna.

Holly berries: Base the berries in Napthol Scarlet with a No. 2 round brush. Add a small comma stroke of Warm White to each berry.

Holly leaves: Base in Jade. Shade the centre with Pine Green, sideloaded in Warm White. Shade the edges of the leaves with Pine Green.

Bells: Paint two coats of Rich Gold, using a No. 2 round brush. Shade with Burnt Sienna.

Violin: Using the No. 4 round brush, paint the violin with two coats of Rich Gold. While wet, shade one side in Burnt Sienna. Paint the top piece with Burnt Sienna and Gold. Shade around the edges with Burnt Sienna. Paint the large S strokes with Burnt Sienna. Outline with Warm White. Use a liner brush to paint the strings Warm White. Outline the top with Warm White.

Finishing: When the design is dry, heat-set. Add Green and Gold Glitz on the violin, poinsettia, leaves, ribbons and bells. Add Gold Glitz to the edges of the ribbon. Sign your T-shirt.

Christmas T-shirt pattern
Enlarge at 200%

CHAPTER 4

GIFTS FOR THE TABLE

LINEN PLACEMATS AND NAPKINS (DEBORAH) (PHOTO PAGE 41)

Paints: Rose Pink, Titanium White, Pine Green, Yellow Oxide, Gold Oxide, Indian Red Oxide, Plaid FolkArt Summer Sky (a light grey-blue). Add Textile Medium to all preceding colours.

Brushes: No. 4 flat brush, No. 2 round brush.

Extras: Plaid FolkArt Thickener.

Preparation: Refer to page 7. Transfer the pattern following the instructions on page 9.

Roses: Base the roses with a mix of Rose Pink and Titanium White and allow to dry. Paint the bowl and petals with a doubleloaded flat brush, using Titanium White and Rose Pink. The throat is Indian Red Oxide. Use a round brush to overstroke the edges of the petals with Titanium White.

Rose leaves: Paint the leaves with a doubleloaded flat brush, using Pine Green and Yellow Oxide.

Orange flowers: With the round brush, paint the petals Gold Oxide. Overstroke with Titanium White. Paint Indian Red Oxide centres with a Yellow Oxide dot. Leaves are Pine Green, diluted with Thickener.

Blue filler flowers: Filler flowers are painted with the round brush. Use doubleloaded dots of Titanium White and Summer Sky.

Finishing: See page 16.

Napkin pattern 100%

Placemat pattern 100%

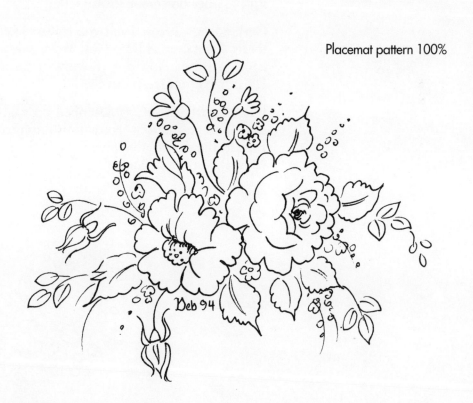

COFFEE CUPS (DEBORAH)
(PHOTO PAGE 41)

Paints: Rose Pink, Titanium White, Pine Green, Yellow Oxide, Gold Oxide, Brown Earth, Dioxazine Purple, Plaid FolkArt Summer Sky (a light grey-blue). Plus Jo Sonja's Glass and Tile Painting Medium added to each colour (see page 15).

Brushes: No. 2 round brush.

Preparation: See page 8.

Roses: The pink rose is based with Rose Pink. Let dry. Then overstroke with Titanium White plus Rose Pink. Throat is Brown Earth with tiny Yellow Oxide dots. The yellow rose is based with a mix of Yellow Oxide and Gold Oxide. Overstroke with Warm White plus Yellow Oxide.

Rose leaves: Leaves are doubleloaded Pine Green and Yellow Oxide.

Blue filler flowers: Summer Sky petals. Yellow Oxide centres. Leaves are painted as for rose leaves, but wipe most of the paint off your brush so that the leaves appear soft.

Purple filler flowers: Dioxazine Purple.

Garland on saucer: Paint the leaves Pine Green. Allow to dry. Paint a small Rose Pink stroke rose in the centre of each scallop. Add dot flowers of Summer Sky and Dioxazine Purple respectively.

Finishing: Heat-set, as described on page 17, following our safety precautions. For a gloss finish to your painting, varnish the design area only with Jo Sonja's Water Based Gloss Polyurethane Varnish.

Pattern 100%
Repeat for saucer

Cup pattern 100%

DESSERT BOWLS (DEBORAH)
(PHOTO PAGE 41)

Paints: As for Coffee Cups.

Brushes: No. 2 round brush.

Preparation: Use the Plastic Hairclip pattern on page 29.

Paint the florals as for the Coffee Cups. As the flowers are smaller, you will need very little detail.

Finishing: As for Coffee Cups.

DONNA'S CHAMPAGNE FLUTE (JUDY)
(PHOTO BACK COVER)

Paints: Liquitex Glossies in Maroon, Pine Green, Red/Orange, White and Gold.

Brushes: No. 4 flat brush, No. 2 flat brush, No. 2 round brush, No. 00 liner brush.

Preparation: See page 7.

Roses: See the colour guide to Judy's float roses on page 70. Mix Maroon, Red/Orange and White and basecoat roses in this colour. Let dry. Then shade centres with a No. 4 flat brush, using the rose base colour with more Maroon added. Add tiny dots of Green and White to the throat with a liner brush.

Leaves: Basecoat with Pine Green. Let dry. Then, using a No. 2 flat brush, paint flat brush leaves. Sideload with Warm White. Paint flat brush leaves as shown in the colour guide on page 70.

Dot daisies: Paint small White dots with the liner brush. Add a pink (rose base colour) centre dot.

Finishing: See page 17.

Champagne Flute pattern 100%

Candle pattern 100%

\\ \\ CANDLE (JUDY) (PHOTO PAGE 41)

Paints: Indian Red Oxide, Warm White, French Blue, Matisse Antique Green.

Brushes: No. 4 flat brush, No. 00 liner brush.

Preparation: See page 8.

Leaves: Use a No. 4 flat brush cornered in Antique Green and sideloaded in Warm White.

Float roses: Corner a No. 4 flat brush into Indian Red Oxide and load Warm White on the other corner. Now paint the petals as shown in the colour guide on page 70. Shade the centres with Indian Red Oxide. Paint tiny dots of Warm White in the throat.

Dot daisies: Make the dots with a liner brush, loaded in French Blue and sideloaded with Warm White. The centre is an Indian Red Oxide dot.
Stems are painted Antique Green with a liner brush.

\\ \\ CANDLESTICK (JUDY) (PHOTO PAGE 41)

Paints: Liquitex Glossies in Black, Yellow, Orange, White and Gold.

Brushes: No. 2 flat brush, No. 2 round brush, No. 00 liner brush.

Leaves: Mix Black into Yellow to make a medium green. Load a No. 2 round brush with this colour and sideload with White.

Roses: Base in Orange plus White. Let dry. Load a No. 2 flat brush with Orange, sideload with White and paint the petals. Refer to the step-by-step guide to float roses on page 70. Float Orange in the centre and add White dots.

Dot daisies: Load a liner brush with Gold and paint dots.

Stems and buds: Paint these with a liner brush – stems are medium green and buds are Orange.

Finishing: None.

Candlestick pattern 100%

GIFTS FOR THE TABLE; COFFEE CUP (PAGE 38) DESSERT BOWL (PAGE 39)
CANDLE AND CANDLESTICK (PAGE 40) PANSY JUG (PAGE 45)
CHAMPAGNE FLUTE (PAGE 39) PLACEMATS AND NAPKIN (PAGE 36)

GIFTS FOR THE CHRISTMAS TABLE: CANDLE (PAGE 48) SUGAR BOWL AND JUG (PAGE 49)
WINE GLASS (PAGE 48) PLACEMAT, NAPKIN AND NAPKIN RING (PAGE 46)

FABRIC-COVERED PHOTO ALBUM (PAGE 53) COFFEE CUP (PAGE 38)
COIN PURSE (PAGE 28) PAINTED PENS (PAGE 55) CANDLESTICK (PAGE 40)

43

GIFTS FOR THE BEDROOM:
PILLOWCASE (PAGE 57) SATIN NIGHTIE (PAGE 59) ATOMISER (PAGE 63)
HEART-SHAPED SACHET (PAGE 60) MIRROR AND HAIRBRUSH (PAGE 61)

With
Love

44

\\ PANSY JUG (DEBORAH) (PHOTO PAGE 41)

Paints: Dioxazine Purple, Titanium White, Yellow Oxide, Pine Green, Gold Oxide. Plus Jo Sonja's Glass and Tile Painting Medium added to each colour (see page 15).

Brushes: No. 2 round brush.

Preparation: See page 8.

Left pansy: Paint the petals with a mix of Dioxazine Purple and Titanium White. Allow to dry. Deepen the base of all petals with straight Dioxazine Purple.

Right pansy: Paint the top petal, as described above. Paint the other petals Yellow Oxide. When dry, deepen the base of the three yellow petals with Dioxazine Purple. Overstroke with Titanium White.

Outline all petals with Titanium White to form frilly edges. Add a Titanium White teardrop stroke to the centre of each pansy. When dry, paint a smaller Gold Oxide dot on top.

Leaves: Doubleloaded Pine Green and Yellow Oxide.

Finishing: Heat-set, as described on page 17, following our safety precautions. For a gloss finish to your painting, varnish the design area only with Jo Sonja's Water based Gloss Polyurethane Varnish.

Pansy Jug pattern 100%

CHAPTER 5

GIFTS FOR THE CHRISTMAS TABLE

Judy has created a whole collection of Christmas gifts to grace the festive table. Some, like the candle, can be painted in minutes. Others will require more time but will certainly be treasured by their recipients.

\ \ LINEN PLACEMATS, NAPKINS AND NAPKIN RINGS (JUDY) (PHOTO PAGE 42)

Paints: Teal Green, Warm White, Jade, Red Earth, Pine Green, Yellow Oxide, Brown Earth, Carbon Black, Smoked Pearl, Rich Gold, White Pearl, Matisse Napthol Scarlet. Add Textile Medium to all preceding colours. Plus Matisse Glitz-a-Matazz in Gold and Green.

Brushes: No. 4 round brush, No. 2 round brush, liner brush.

Preparation: Follow the instructions for transferring patterns to fabric on page 9 and fabric preparation page 7.

Napkin pattern 100%

Bonbon: Basecoat with No. 4 round brush in Smoked Pearl. Do the ribbon at the same time. When dry, paint two coats of White Pearl. Tint with Rich Gold at the end. Ribbons are two coats of Napthol Scarlet. Add Brown Earth to the red and shade the ribbons. Using the liner brush, outline the bows with Rich Gold. Shade the top and bottom of the bows with Green and Gold Glitz-a-Matazz. Add Green Glitz around the bonbon.

Bow: Give the bow two coats of Teal Green using the No. 4 round brush. Highlight with White Pearl. Add tiny lines in Napthol Scarlet, Warm White and Rich Gold. Add a line of Gold Glitz around the bow.

Judy. 1994

Holly: Base in Pine Green. Add Rich Gold lines with a liner brush. Add extra strokes of Rich Gold. Acorns are light brown (mix Warm White and Brown Earth). Add small strokes with a No. 2 round brush, loaded in Brown Earth and sideloaded with Warm White. Holly berries are two coats of Napthol Scarlet. Tint the edges of the berries with Jade. Add a Warm White comma stroke highlight and a Carbon Black dot on top.

Extra strokes around the design are painted with a liner brush in Pine Green and Rich Gold. Add Green and Gold Glitz accents.

Bells: Base with two coats of Rich Gold. Add Brown Earth strokes with a liner brush. Shade with Brown Earth. Add accents of Gold and Green Glitz.

Candle: Base with two coats of Napthol Scarlet. Add Warm White at the top. The flame is Red Earth, with a stroke of Yellow Oxide. Add Warm White lines around the flame.

Maintenance: Heat-set fabric items. Handwash.

Napkin Ring
pattern 100%

Judy. 1993

Placemat pattern
Enlarge at 140%

Judy. 1994

❧ CANDLE (JUDY) (PHOTO PAGE 42)

Paints: Napthol Crimson, Pine Green, Brown Earth.

Brushes: No. 2 round brush.

Preparation: See page 8. If you are in a hurry, you can paint directly onto the wax, using artists' acrylics or acrylic enamels. Freehand the holly sprig, using the holly pattern opposite as a guide.

Paint the holly berries Napthol Crimson. Leave a little gap in each to create a highlight. Leaves are Pine Green. Stems are Brown Earth.

Candle pattern 100%

❧❧ WINE GLASS (JUDY) (PHOTO PAGE 42)

Paints: Pine Green, Teal Green, Indian Red Oxide, Yellow Oxide, Red Earth, Rich Gold, Warm White, Matisse Napthol Scarlet. Jo Sonja's Glass and Tile Painting Medium.

Brushes: No. 2 round brush, No. 00 liner brush.

Extras: Sponge.

Preparation: See page 7.

Holly wreath: Load a No. 2 round brush in Pine Green and a touch of Teal Green. Sideload with Rich Gold. Paint the leaves. Add extra leaves of straight Rich Gold. When dry, paint Napthol Scarlet berries with a Warm White dot on each.

Candles: Load the No. 2 round brush with Indian Red Oxide and paint the candles. The flame is a Yellow Oxide stroke. Shade the flame with Red Earth. Add small strokes of Rich Gold around the flame.

Wine Glass pattern
Enlarge at 140%

Judy. 1994.

Ribbon: Same as for the Sugar Bowl and Jug below, but use Indian Red Oxide instead of Napthol Scarlet.

Sponging: Add Rich Gold sponging as for the Jug (below). When dry, tie a ribbon around the stem of the glass and place in tissue in a gift box. Do not paint rim.

Finishing: See page 17 for heat-setting instructions. For a gloss finish, varnish the painted areas.

\ \ SUGAR BOWL AND JUG (JUDY)
(PHOTO PAGE 42)

Paints: Teal Green, Rich Gold, Warm White, Pine Green, Matisse Napthol Scarlet. Matisse Glitz-a-Matazz in Green.

Brushes: No. 4 round brush, No. 2 round brush, No. 00 liner brush.

Preparation: See pages 7 and 15.

Bow and ribbon for bells: Using a No. 2 round brush, base with two coats of Napthol Scarlet. Add a border around the bottom of the bowl and jug of fine Napthol Scarlet strokes to suggest ribbon.

Leaves: Paint the small leaves with a No. 2 round brush loaded in Pine Green and sideloaded in Rich Gold.

Bells: Load a No. 4 round brush with Pine Green and basecoat the bells. Outline the bell in Rich Gold with your liner brush and add fine strokes to the bottom of the bell. To create a snow effect on the tops of the bells and on the ribbons, paint generously with Warm White.

Holly: Load a No. 2 round brush with Pine Green and sideload with Rich Gold to paint the leaves. The holly berries are painted Napthol Scarlet with a liner brush. Paint a Warm White dot on top of each berry.

Sponging: Sponge the handle and tops and bottoms of the jug and bowl with Rich Gold. Avoid the pouring lip.

Sugar Bowl pattern
Enlarge at 140%

Judy. 1993.

CHAPTER 6

GIFTS TO TREASURE

Chain and discount stores abound with inexpensive picture frames that can be transformed into heirlooms by adding painted flowers. Cheap plastic photo albums can also become special gifts when painted with a monogram and folk art design.

FLANNEL FLOWER FRAME (DEBORAH)
(PHOTO PAGE 21)

Deborah painted this frame as a gift for her aunts, Philomena and Bette. The photo is of their father (and Deborah's grandfather), Edwin Hill, a World War I veteran.

Paints: Titanium White, Teal Green.

Brushes: No. 2 round brush.

Flannel Flower Frame pattern 100%

Extras: Soft cloth.

Preparation: None. Deborah painted directly onto the pine frame.

Flannel flowers: Paint the petals and centres Titanium White. Let dry. Paint a soft wash of Titanium White plus a little Teal Green around the base of the petals. Blot with a cotton bud if the colour is too strong. Paint dots of this light Teal Green colour on the centres.

Leaves and stems: Titanium White with Teal Green. Doubleload this colour with Titanium White and paint comma stroke leaves and fine stems.

Edges of frame: Rub a watery mix of Titanium White plus Teal Green around the edges of the frame.

Finishing: Varnish if desired.

COTTAGE FLOWER FRAME (DEBORAH) (PHOTO PAGE 21)

Deborah carried through the theme of the cottage garden in this sepia photo of her mother as a child and painted a swag of cottage flowers on the frame.

Paints: Teal Green, Rose Pink, Warm White, Indian Red Oxide, Pine Green, Yellow Oxide, Plaid FolkArt Summer Sky (a light grey-blue).

Brushes: No. 2 round brush.

Preparation: The frame was made of limed pine. Deborah basepainted the front with Teal Green but left the mouldings in the original finish.

Roses: Doubleloaded Rose Pink and Warm White stroke roses. Indian Red Oxide throats, dotted with Yellow Oxide.

Blue flowers: Summer Sky petals. Yellow Oxide centres.

Leaves: Doubleloaded Pine Green and Yellow Oxide.

Cottage Flower Frame
pattern 100%
Reverse for opposite corner

\ \ KEEPSAKES BOOK (DEBORAH)
(PHOTO PAGE 21)

You can pick up fabric-covered books from folk art and craft shops. Alternatively, you could cover a notebook with an appropriately sized rectangular linen doily or table runner. Add your friend's initials to the centre of the design.

Paints: Rose Pink, Titanium White, Pine Green, Yellow Oxide, Ultramarine, Carbon Black, Brown Earth. Add Textile Medium to each colour.

Brushes: No. 2 round brush, No. 6 flat brush, No. 00 liner brush.

Extras: Plaid FolkArt Thickener.

Preparation: No preparation. Transfer the pattern with a fabric transfer pencil, as explained on page 9. Use a lettering book as a reference for the initials.

Background wash: Wet the area around the roses and flowers with Thickener. Mix Pine Green, Yellow Oxide and a touch of Ultramarine with Thickener to make a transparent colour. It should be very soft and subtle. Paint this mix over the area where the design will go. Make the wash very light where it blends into the white fabric.

Roses: Base with a mix of Rose Pink and Titanium White. Allow to dry. With a doubleloaded (Rose Pink and Titanium White) flat brush, paint the petals and bowl. Using a round brush, overstroke the edges of the petals with Titanium White. The throat is floated in with a flat brush, using Brown Earth. Add Yellow Oxide dots.

Rose leaves: Doubleloaded Pine Green and Yellow Oxide with either a round or a flat brush, whichever method you are most comfortable with. Mix a little Carbon Black into the Pine Green for some of the leaves.

Blue flowers: Flowers are Titanium White plus Ultramarine plus a touch of Yellow Oxide. Brush-mix these colours to paint the petals. When dry, add a Yellow Oxide centre, partly outlined with a crescent of Brown Earth.

Initials: Using a liner brush, base the initials with Pine Green.

Finishing: When the book is dry, you may wish to spray it with Scotchgard®.

Keepsakes Book
pattern 100%

\\ FABRIC-COVERED PHOTO ALBUM (JUDY)
(PHOTO PAGE 43)

Paints: Dioxazine Purple, Red Earth, Burnt Sienna, Carbon Black, Yellow Oxide, Warm White, Smoked Pearl. Add Textile Medium to all paints.

Brushes: No. 4 flat brush, No. 2 round brush, No. 2 round brush, No. 00 liner brush.

Preparation: Transfer pattern following the instructions on page 9.

Leaves: Mix a little Carbon Black into Yellow Oxide to make a dark green. Load this colour onto a No. 4 flat brush and sideload with Warm White. Paint flat brush leaves as shown in the colour guide on page 70.

Float roses: Make a pale apricot by mixing Warm White, Burnt Sienna and Red Earth. Use a No. 4 flat brush doubleloaded with pale apricot and Warm White to paint the petals. See the guide on page 70.

Buds: Paint the buds using the same method as the float roses, but use a No. 2 flat brush.

Violets: Basecoat all petals with Smoked Pearl. Load a No. 2 round brush with Dioxazine Purple. Paint the top petal. Load the brush with Dioxazine Purple and sideload with Warm White for the two side petals. Face the White side of the brush towards the top. Paint the bottom petal the same way. The centre is Red Earth with a Warm White dot underneath. Paint a cream comma (Warm White plus Yellow Oxide) on either side of the centre. Shade all petals near the centre with Dioxazine Purple.

Dot daisies: Dot daisies are painted with a No. 2 round brush and Dioxazine Purple or pale apricot (the rose colour).

Wash leaves: Paint soft, wash leaves (see page 14 for washes on fabric) of Yellow Oxide plus a touch of Carbon Black around the edges of the design.

Finishing: You can add a bow, tassel or charm for that special finishing touch.

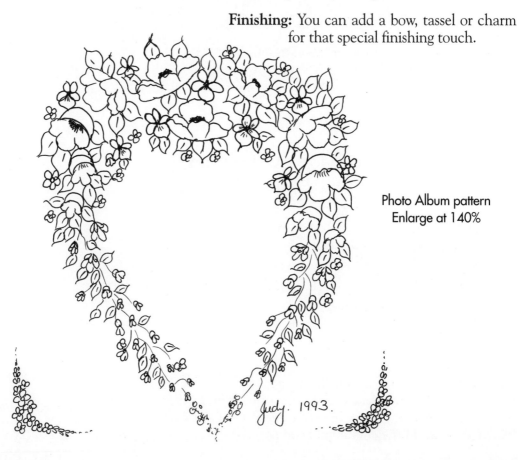

Photo Album pattern
Enlarge at 140%

\\ PAINTED PENS (JUDY) (PHOTO PAGE 43)

For a lovely personalised gift, have the recipient's name engraved on the pen. This should be done prior to painting. Rich Gold paint can be rubbed into the engraved area, if desired. Judy painted the burgundy engraved pen in our photo as a gift for Deborah several years ago.

Paints: Indian Red Oxide, French Blue, Warm White, Matisse Antique Green.

Brushes: No. 2 flat brush, No. 2 round brush, No. 00 liner brush.

Leaves: Paint tiny leaves using a No. 2 round brush, loaded in Antique Green and sideloaded in Warm White.

Float Roses: Refer to the colour worksheet on page 70. Doubleload a No. 2 flat brush with Indian Red Oxide on one side and Warm White on the other. Paint the rose petals. Float Indian Red Oxide in the centre. Add Warm White dots to the throats with a liner brush.

Dot daisies: Load a liner brush with French Blue and sideload into Warm White. Paint the dots.
   Add Antique Green stems and Indian Red Oxide buds.

Finishing: Remove the top of the pen. Judy paints two or three coats of water-based satin varnish over the whole pen, then a further six coats over the painted area only. Each coat must be dry before the next is applied. Do not replace the top until the varnish has cured (about four weeks) or the pen and top will stick together. A tassel attached to the end of the pen adds a special touch.

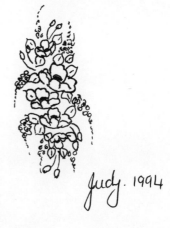

Pens patterns 100%

PAINTED GLASS SHOES (DEBORAH)
(PHOTO PAGE 21)

Deborah's mother found the purple glass slipper (unpainted) in a shop on Cape Cod, in the United States and brought it back as a gift for Deborah who has a collection of ornamental shoes and shoe lasts. Deborah discovered the pink shoe in a second-hand shop in the Southern Highlands of New South Wales. You could decorate any coloured glass object (vases, bowls, etc) with these tiny florals. Adjust the colours to show up against your background.

Paints: Rose Pink, Warm White, Titanium White, Ultramarine, Pine Green, Yellow Oxide, Dioxazine Purple, Gold Oxide. Plus Jo Sonja's Glass and Tile Painting Medium added to each colour.

Brushes: No 1 or 2 round brush.

Preparation: See page 7.

Roses: These roses are so tiny that you need very little detail, just a few strokes. Base in Rose Pink plus Warm White. Let dry. Overstroke with Titanium White. Add an Indian Red Oxide throat.

Blue flowers: Ultramarine plus Titanium White petals. Yellow Oxide centres.

Violets: Dioxazine Purple plus Titanium White petals. Gold Oxide dot at the centre.

White dot flowers: Titanium White dot petals. Gold Oxide centres.

Leaves and stems: Doubleloaded Pine Green and Warm White.

Finishing: Heat-set with a hairdryer, if desired.

Glass Shoe pattern 100%

CHAPTER 7

GIFTS FOR THE BEDROOM AND BATHROOM

Y ou will find plenty of items to decorate for the bedroom or bathroom. Imagine a white battenburg lace cushion or pillow adorned with painted roses. And a matching lingerie bag or even a painted silk nightie or bathrobe. Other projects might include a handpainted hairbrush and comb, painted make-up brushes, soap holders, even painted soap!

\ \ \ PILLOWCASE (JUDY) (PHOTO PAGE 44)

Paints: Matisse Antique Green (or Teal Green and Fawn mixed), Red Earth, Dioxazine Purple, Warm White, Yellow Oxide, Burnt Sienna, Smoked Pearl. Add Textile Medium to the preceding colours.

Brushes: No. 4 flat brush, No. 2 flat brush, No. 2 round brush, No. 00 liner brush.

Preparation: Read the section on fabric preparation and fabric painting, pages 7 and 13, and remember to place a piece of cardboard covered in plastic wrap inside the pillowcase.

Roses: Basecoat the roses with Smoked Pearl first.

Rose No. 1, mix Red Earth and Warm White. Sideload a No. 4 flat brush into this mix and load the other side of the brush with Warm White. Blend on a tile. Refer to the colour step-by-step guide on page 70. Using a wriggling motion, proceed to paint the rose. Pick up fresh paint for each section of the rose. This will give extra depth and texture.

Rose No. 2, mix Dioxazine Purple and Warm White. Load this mixture on one side of your brush and Warm White on the other. Paint as for Rose No. 1.

Shade the centres of the roses with Burnt Sienna. When dry, doubleload a liner brush with Antique Green and Warm White and paint tiny dots in the centres.

Leaves: Refer to the step-by-step guide on page 70. Using a No. 4 flat brush, sideload into Warm White on one side and Antique Green on the other, then blend. Vary the leaf colours by occasionally doubleloading with Warm White on one side and a mix of Antique Green and Burnt Sienna on the other side. In addition, paint some soft wash leaves around the outside of the pattern (see page 14 for information about washes on fabric).

Large buds: Using the same mix as the roses, load a No. 4 flat brush and sideload with Warm White. You do not need to basecoat the buds first. Reload the brush regularly.

Smaller buds: Use a No. 2 flat brush and the same technique as for the larger buds. The colours are Dioxazine Purple and Warm White.

All the stems for the buds are painted with a liner brush, using Antique Green plus Warm White.

Dot daisies: Refer to the step-by-step colour guide on page 70. Using a No. 2 round brush, paint five dots, pressing down, then lifting up. Add a dot of Yellow Oxide in the centre and a fine line under the Yellow Oxide dot.

Finishing and maintenance: See page 16.

Pillowcase pattern
Enlarge at 140%

\ \ \ CUTWORK PILLOW (DEBORAH)
(PHOTO PAGE 24)

Paints: Warm White, Yellow Oxide, Napthol Crimson, Red Earth, Indian Red Oxide, Brown Earth, Pine Green, Plaid FolkArt Summer Sky (a light grey-blue). Add Textile Medium to all preceding colours.

Brushes: No. 2 round brush, No. 6 flat brush for floated shading.

Preparation: Remove the pillow. Pre-wash and dry the linen cover, following the instructions on page 7. Place a piece of cardboard covered in plastic wrap inside the cover to protect the back.

Use the pattern and paint as for the Canvas Hatbox flowers on page 25.

Finishing: Heat-set (page 16).

\ \ SATIN NIGHTIE (JUDY)
(PHOTO PAGE 44)

Paints: Indian Red Oxide, Warm White, Carbon Black and Yellow Oxide. Add Textile Medium to all the preceding colours.

Brushes: No. 4 flat brush, No. 2 flat brush, No. 2 round brush, No. 00 liner brush.

Preparation: Read the instructions on page 7.

Buds: Refer to the step-by-step guide on page 70. With a No. 4 flat brush, paint the larger buds Indian Red Oxide, sideloaded with Warm White. Use a No. 2 flat brush and the same method for the smaller buds.

Leaves and stems: Leaves are painted with the No. 2 round brush. Mix a medium green with Yellow Oxide plus Carbon Black. Load the green mixture on your brush and sideload into Warm White. Stems are painted with a liner brush in the same colours.

Finishing and maintenance: Heat-set as described on page 16. Do not allow the iron to touch the fabric itself. Handwash.

Satin Nightie
pattern 100%

⧹⧹ HEART-SHAPED POT POURRI SACHET (JUDY) (PHOTO PAGE 44)

Paints: Red Earth, Warm White, Dioxazine Purple, Carbon Black, Yellow Oxide. Add Textile Medium to these colours.

Brushes: No. 4 flat brush, No. 2 round brush, No. 00 liner brush.

Preparation: No preparation except to slip a small sheet of plastic-wrapped cardboard inside the heart to protect the back.

Roses: Paint as for the Mirror on page 61.

Filler flowers: Mix a medium purple with Dioxazine Purple and Warm White. Load a No. 2 round brush with this colour and sideload into Warm White. Paint a number of small dot daisies around the design, picking up extra paint as you go.

Leaves: Mix a medium green with Yellow Oxide plus Carbon Black. Load a No. 2 round brush with this mixture and sideload with Warm White.

Finishing: Fill with pot pourri. Glue on gold charm with craft glue.

Pot Pourri pattern 100%

Judy. 1994.

HAIRBRUSH AND HAND MIRROR (JUDY)
(PHOTO PAGE 44)

Paints: Dioxazine Purple, Red Earth, Warm White, Rich Gold, Pine Green.

Brushes: No. 2 round brush, No. 4 flat brush, No. 00 liner brush.

Pansy buds: Use a No. 2 round brush and Dioxazine Purple plus Warm White (medium purple). Shade with Dioxazine Purple. Outline with Rich Gold, using a liner brush.

Roses and buds: Use a No. 2 round brush and combinations of Red Earth and Warm White. Add extra Warm White to one side of each bud to highlight it.

Stems: Stems are painted with a liner brush and Pine Green, sideloaded with Rich Gold.

Dot daisies: With a liner brush, paint tiny dot daisies on the handle of the mirror. Use the rose and pansy colours on your palette.

Wash leaves: Paint watery Pine Green leaves with a No. 2 round brush.

Edges: When the painting is completed, sideload a No. 4 flat brush, and float a soft wash of Dioxazine Purple around the edges of the brush and mirror.

HINT: Pre-wet the edges before floating.

Finishing: Varnish the painted area with water-based matte or satin varnish.

Hairbrush pattern 100%

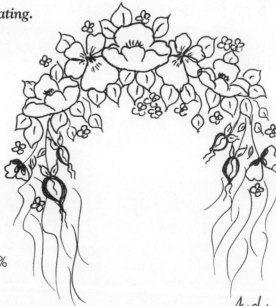

Mirror pattern 100%

GREEN PERFUME BOTTLE (JUDY)
(PHOTO PAGE 21)

Paints: Yellow Oxide, Warm White, Red Earth, Dioxazine Purple, Pine Green. Add 3 parts Jo Sonja's Glass and Tile Painting Medium to 1 part of each colour.

Brushes: No. 1 round brush, No. 00 liner brush.

Preparation: Clean glass (page 7). This pattern can be freehanded as it is very simple. Have Judy's pattern close by as a guide.

Leaves and stems: Load the round brush with Pine Green and sideload with Warm White. Paint all small leaves. Stems are painted the same way, but with a liner brush.

Pansy: Basecoat top petals with Yellow Oxide. Other petals are Dioxazine Purple. Let dry. Shade yellow petals with Dioxazine Purple and purple petals with Yellow Oxide. Paint a small Red Earth dot at the centre, with Warm White commas on either side. Paint a Warm White dot just under the centre, using a liner brush.

Small flowers: Base each petal with two coats of Warm White. Shade the centre with Yellow Oxide. With the liner brush, paint small dots of Pine Green mixed with Warm White at the centre.

Ribbon: Load the liner brush with Yellow Oxide and sideload in Warm White.

Dot daisies: With the liner brush, paint small dot flowers of Yellow Oxide, sideloaded in Warm White. Paint these daisies on top of the ribbon.

Keep repeating the pattern around the bottle.

Finishing: Heat-set when dry, bearing in mind our safety warnings (page 17).

Perfume Bottle
pattern 100%

ATOMISER (JUDY) (PHOTO PAGE 44)

Paints: Warm White, Turner's Yellow, Burnt Sienna, Dioxazine Purple, Rich Gold, Pine Green, Indian Red Oxide, Opal. Add 3 parts Jo Sonja's Glass and Tile Painting Medium to 1 part of each colour.

Brushes: No. 1 round brush, No. 2 round brush, No. 00 liner brush.

Preparation: Clean glass (page 7). This pattern can be freehanded as it is very simple. Have Judy's pattern close by as a guide.
   All work is done with a No. 2 round brush, unless otherwise stated.

Butterflies: Paint all the butterflies using the method described for No. 1. Bodies are Burnt Sienna, highlighted with Rich Gold. With the liner brush, outline each wing in Rich Gold. Feelers are also Rich Gold.

No. 1 Base the wings with two coats of Warm White. Shade wings with Dioxazine Purple.

No. 2 wings: Turner's Yellow. Shade and decorate with Red Earth.

No. 3 wings: Opal. Shade and decorate with Indian Red Oxide.

No. 4 wings: Warm White. Shade and decorate with Dioxazine Purple.

Leaves: Load the No. 1 round brush with Pine Green and sideload with Warm White.

Filler flowers: Outer flowers are Opal. Centre flowers are Warm White. Shade all petals with Indian Red Oxide. Centres are Turner's Yellow. With a liner brush, outline all petals with Indian Red Oxide.

Dot daisies: Warm White with Indian Red Oxide centres.

Finishing: Heat-set when dry, bearing in mind our safety warnings (page 17).

Atomiser pattern 100%

Judy. 1994.

CHAPTER 8

GIFTS FOR THE GARDEN

Wet gardener could resist a handpainted sun umbrella to shelter from the hot sun and her own special chair in which to sit and survey her gardening accomplishments.

⟍⟍ UMBRELLA (JUDY) (PHOTO PAGE 69)

Paints: Dioxazine Purple, Indian Red Oxide, Warm White, French Blue, Carbon Black, Yellow Oxide, Pine Green. Textile Medium.

Brushes: No. 6 flat brush, No. 4 flat brush, No. 2 flat brush, No. 4 round brush, No. 00 liner brush.

Preparation: Trace on the pattern with white transfer paper. Note that the pattern needs to be repeated.

Purple petunias: Mix Dioxazine Purple and Warm White to form a medium purple. With a No. 4 round brush paint the petunia, reloading for each section. While the base colour is wet, add extra Warm White to the edges of the petals and blend down towards the centre. Shade the base of the petunia petals using the base colour with more Dioxazine Purple added. Centres are painted Warm White and Yellow Oxide with a liner brush. Add Warm White dots.

Pink petunias: The pink petunias are based in Indian Red Oxide plus Warm White to make a medium pink. Extra Indian Red Oxide is added at the base of the petals. Otherwise, paint as for the purple petunias.

Stems: Pine Green plus Warm White.

Roses: Use the No. 6 flat brush for the larger roses and the No. 4 flat brush for the smaller roses. See the colour guide on page 70. The roses are Indian Red Oxide, sideloaded in Warm White.

Buds: With a No. 4 flat brush, paint the buds in the colours of the petunias and roses.

Waterdrops: Paint with watery Warm White. Allow to dry, then outline finely with straight Warm White. Add a tiny Warm White highlight. See page 71 for a step-by-step guide.

Finishing: Heat-set the painted area with a hairdryer.

Umbrella pattern
Enlarge at 200%

Judy. 1994

\ \ \ Director's Chair Cover (Judy)
(photo page 69)

Judy has transformed this old director's chair by painting new canvas covers. They make great gifts for friends, particularly if you use colours to co-ordinate with their house.

Paints: Burnt Sienna, Yellow Oxide, Warm White, Dioxazine Purple, Red Earth, Turner's Yellow, Carbon Black, Pine Green, Teal Green, Fawn, Smoked Pearl.

Brushes: No. 6 flat brush, No. 4 flat brush, No. 4 round brush, No. 2 round brush.

Preparation: Remove canvas covers from chair. Use white graphite transfer paper to transfer the design.

Large leaves: Basecoat all large leaves with two coats of a mix of Teal Green and Fawn. When dry, load a No. 4 round brush with the green mix and sideload with Warm White. Face the Warm White corner of the brush towards the leaf. Start from the top of the leaf and use a press-down, lift-up method to half way down the leaf. This is called 'turning' the leaf. With a dry brush, highlight the leaves with a little Warm White. Shade the bases of the leaves with Teal Green.

Poppy leaves: Basecoat with Pine Green. When dry, load the No. 2 round brush with Pine Green and sideload with Yellow Oxide. Stroke down the leaf.

Iris: Basecoat with Smoked Pearl. Using a No. 4 round brush, paint the petals medium purple (Dioxazine Purple and Warm White mix). Paint each petal separately. While wet, run Warm White around the edge of the petal and drag into the petal. Shade the base of the petals with Dioxazine Purple. The centre is Yellow Oxide. With a dry brush, softly highlight under the centre with Warm White. Add some fine strokes of Dioxazine Purple.

Poppy: Basecoat with Red Earth. Let dry. Using a No. 6 flat brush, load into Red Earth and sideload into Turner's Yellow. Paint over each petal. Float Carbon Black shading in the centre. When dry, add tiny dots of Yellow Oxide and Warm White at the centre.

Poppy buds: Using a No. 4 flat brush, basecoat in Red Earth. Let dry. Load in Red Earth and sideload in Turner's Yellow. Paint over the bud.

Tulip: Basecoat with Smoked Pearl. Allow to dry. Using a No. 4 round brush, paint each petal Turner's Yellow. While wet, run Warm White around the tops of each petal and drag down into the petal.

Tulip buds: Base the buds in Smoked Pearl with a No. 4 round brush. While wet, add Yellow Oxide shading and run Warm White around the top and drag down into the petal.

Stems: All stems are painted in Teal Green and Fawn mix, sideloaded with Teal. Use a No. 4 round brush.

Bird: Refer to step-by-step guide on page 71. Basecoat with Smoked Pearl. Using a No. 4 round brush, load in Yellow Oxide and sideload in Warm White.

Filler flowers: Add a variety of dot daisies in and out of the pattern. Use the colours on your palette.

Chair Cover pattern Enlarge at 200%

Judy. 1993.

\ \ GARDENING TOOLS (JUDY)
(PHOTO PAGE 69)

Paints: Smoked Pearl, Dioxazine Purple, Pine Green, Burnt Sienna, Warm White, Yellow Oxide.

Brushes: No. 4 flat brush, No. 2 flat brush, No. 2 round brush.

Preparation: Basecoat the handles with Smoked Pearl.

Leaves: Load a No. 4 flat brush with Pine Green and sideload with Warm White. Every now and then, doubleload Pine Green and Burnt Sienna on one side and corner into Warm White on the other. Paint watery versions of these leaves at the outside of the design.

Lilac flowers: Load a No. 2 flat brush with Dioxazine Purple and sideload with Warm White. Make tiny strokes, picking up extra Warm White as you go. Make the other lilac lighter by mixing extra Warm White into the purple.

Dot daisies: Using a No. 2 round brush, paint 5 Warm White dots forming a circle for the daisy. Paint a Yellow Oxide dot in the centre of each daisy.

Finishing: Varnish with at least six coats of water-based satin varnish.

Gardening Tools
pattern 100%

Judy. 1993.

GIFTS FOR THE GARDEN: UMBRELLA (PAGE 64)
DIRECTOR'S CHAIR COVER (PAGE 66) GARDENING TOOLS (PAGE 68)

69

STEP-BY-STEP COLOUR WORKSHEETS

70

Judy. 1994.

STEP-BY-STEP COLOUR WORKSHEETS

GIFTS FOR BABIES AND KIDS:
BABY'S SATIN SHOES (PAGE 76) TEDDY T-SHIRT (PAGE 74)
CHRISTENING MUG AND EGG CUP (PAGE 73) GIFT TAGS (PAGE 77)

72

CHAPTER 9

GIFTS FOR BABIES AND KIDS

Here are some wonderful ideas for gifts for babies and small children. All the items are inexpensive to buy – the egg cup cost less than a dollar – but they all become special when handpainted.

CHRISTENING MUG AND EGG CUP (DEBORAH) (PHOTO PAGE 72)

Egg Cup pattern 100%

Paints: Pine Green, Yellow Oxide, Raw Sienna, Brown Earth, Carbon Black, Plaid FolkArt Summer Sky (a light grey-blue), Napthol Crimson. Add Jo Sonja's Glass and Tile Painting Medium to the preceding colours.

Brushes: No. 2 round brush.

Extras: Jo Sonja's Gloss Polyurethane Varnish.

Preparation: Wipe clean.

Paint the teddy bear as for the Teddy T-shirt below. Paint soft clouds of Summer Sky. Paint a thin coat of Pine Green under the teddy. Add Napthol Crimson tulips on Pine Green stems.

Finishing and maintenance: Heat-set in an oven, if desired, but follow our safety procedures on page 17. Alternatively, heat-set with a hairdryer. Varnish the painted areas with Jo Sonja's Gloss Polyurethane Varnish. These pieces should be gently handwashed only.

Christening Mug
pattern 100%

Deborah 93

\ \ TEDDY T-SHIRT (DEBORAH)
(PHOTO PAGE 72)

Paints: Warm White, Pine Green, Yellow Oxide, Raw Sienna, Brown Earth, Carbon Black, Plaid FolkArt Summer Sky (a light grey-blue). Add Textile Medium to the preceding colours.

Brushes: No. 2 round brush, No. 6 flat brush.

Extras: Thickener. Dimensional paint in Light Blue, Red and Green.

Preparation: Read pages 7 and 13 on preparing and painting fabric. Because this T-shirt is so small, you will need to cut a special shirt board out of cardboard, cover with plastic wrap and place inside the shirt.

Transfer the pattern according to the instructions on page 9.

Sky and foreground: Using the No. 6 flat brush, wet the sky area with Thickener and paint a wash of Summer Sky. Allow to dry and add Warm White clouds. Use the same technique to paint the wash in the foreground. The colour is Pine Green plus Yellow Oxide. Use plenty of Thickener on the foreground area before painting and add water (not too much!) to the paint. Let dry.

Teddy bear: Base the bear with the round brush and Yellow Oxide plus a little Raw Sienna. Lighten the snout by mixing in some Warm White to the fur colour. Add other highlights as shown in the photo. Outline the bear with tiny Brown Earth lines to suggest scruffy fur. Eyes and nose are Carbon Black, painted with a liner brush. Leave a little gap of white fabric showing in the eyes and the nose to create highlights. The mouth is Brown Earth.

Finishing: When the underlying colours are dry, heat-set, as described on page 16. Now, add clouds, grass, flowers and bow with dimensional paint. Be careful not to smudge the paint. Dimensional paint can take at least 24 hours to dry when used on fabric.

Teddy pattern
Enlarge at 125%

BABY'S SATIN SHOES (DEBORAH)
(PHOTO PAGE 72)

Paints: Yellow Oxide, Warm White, Napthol Crimson, Pine Green, Plaid FolkArt Summer Sky (a light grey-blue). Add Textile Medium to the preceding colours.

Brushes: No. 2 round brush.

Preparation: No preparation is required. Paint directly onto the shoes.

Flowers: Paint the central rose doubleloaded Napthol Crimson and Warm White. Paint the two outer roses doubleloaded Yellow Oxide and Warm White. Daisies are Summer Sky. Leaves are Pine Green plus Yellow Oxide.

Baby's Shoe pattern 100%

CHAPTER 10

GIFT TAGS

Handpainted gift tags to match your gift add a special touch and are quick and inexpensive to make. We use watercolour paper or thin cardboard – not too thick or it is difficult to cut and fold.

Transfer the pattern by placing the paper against a well-lit window and slipping the pattern underneath. Check that placement is correct. Then secure paper and pattern to the glass with Scotch Magic Tape. Trace the outlines lightly onto the paper with a lead pencil. Paint your design as you would on any other surface but do remember mistakes and smudges cannot be removed, only camouflaged. The paint will also dry very quickly on paper. Make a hole in the corner with a hole punch and add a gold thread or ribbon.

Here are some patterns for gift tags to get you started.

Gift Tag patterns 100%

Happy
Birthday!

Gift Tag Patterns 100%

Happy
Christening!

CHAPTER 11

PERSONALISING GIFTS WITH LETTERING AND MONOGRAMS

Make your painted gifts very special by adding a name or monogram. You don't need to be good at lettering to do this. We often cheat and take suitable pieces to the engraver. Glass items such as the Champagne Flute (page 41) can be engraved, as can pens (see the Painted Pens on page 43). Engraving should be done prior to painting your design.

You can also experiment with lettering stencils or, if you are working on a hard surface, try Letraset self-adhesive letters, available from newsagents and art suppliers. You can make these look as if you have done them yourself by carefully painting over the letters. Where appropriate, the letters can then be varnished.

If you want to try some actual lettering, there are many good lettering books to use as a guide. Use paint and a liner brush or one of the commercial liner tools, which include the Fluid Writer pen by Kemper Tool Inc. and the DecoWriter Tip which fits onto DecoArt paints.

Dimensional paint can also be used to create letters. It can be used on wood as well as fabric. Experiment with dimensional paint on fabric to simulate embroidered initials.

On paper (such as gift tags) Deborah uses felt-tip calligraphy pens available from newsagents. They are inexpensive, simple and quick to use and produce very acceptable results. The easiest alphabet to copy is italics which you can find in most lettering books. Practise varying the pressure you apply – downstrokes should be thicker. You will find a variety of alphabets and inscriptions to incorporate into your folk art gifts in Deborah's book *The Craft Collection of Verses & Alphabets* (Deborah Kneen Studios).

ABOUT THE AUTHORS

JUDY ALLEN

Judy Allen is a folk and decorative artist, well known for her innovative painting on a variety of surfaces, including wearable art. A popular teacher, Judy has also exhibited her work successfully at the prestigious Australian Craft Show. She is a regular contributor to *Folk Art and Decorative Painting* and *Australian Country Craft*. Judy lives in Sydney with her husband and four children.

DEBORAH KNEEN

Deborah Kneen is the author of numerous bestselling books on decorative painting and craft in general. Her distinctive folk art has been featured in more than 50 articles in Australian and American magazines. Deborah is editorial consultant and columnist for *Folk Art and Decorative Painting*. In 1995 she became the first Australian artist to be represented in the permanent collection of the American Society of Decorative Painters.

Back cover picture: *Canvas Hatbox (page 25), Cottage Flower Frame (page 51), Donna's Champagne Flute (page 39), Baby's Satin Shoes (page 76), Evening Bag (page 27), Painted Pen (page 55), Brooch (page 29)*